MW00860998

HAYDN
THE COMPLETE PIANO SONATAS

EDITED BY MAURICE HINSON

ABOUT THIS EDITION

Alfred has made every effort to make this book not only attractive, but more convenient and long-lasting as well. Most books larger than 96 pages do not lie flat or stay open easily. In addition, the pages in these books (which are usually glued together) tend to break away from the spine after repeated use.

In Alfred's special **lay-flat binding** editions for large books, pages are sewn together in multiples of 16, preventing pages from falling out of the book while still allowing it to stay open easily. Alfred also offers another type of special binding for large books called **plastic comb binding**. This format allows the book to lie open even flatter than the lay-flat binding.

We hope that these long-lasting, convenient bindings will encourage additional use of our publications and will continue to bring added pleasure to you for years to come.

HAYDN
THE COMPLETE PIANO SONATAS
VOLUME I

Maurice Hinson, Editor

CONTENTS

This edition is dedicated with admiration and appreciation to Malcolm Bilson.

Maurice Hinson

Thematic Index

Foreword

Haydn's contribution to piano literature is very large and totals more than 150 pieces, including solo works as well as concertos, trios, quartets, and other ensemble compositions employing piano parts. To understand the significance of Haydn's piano works in relation to his entire compositional output we must first briefly discuss his biographical background and the social environments for which these pieces were created.

Haydn (1732–1809) grew up in a home where there was no piano, but there was a primitive harp with which his father, a farmer and wheelwright who liked to sing, accompanied himself. Haydn, who had a beautiful voice, actually began his career as a choirboy and developed facility both at the keyboard and with the violin. He was not as fortunate as the sons of Johann Sebastian Bach to receive systematic and methodical musical instruction. He lacked a musical mentor of the stature of Leopold Mozart, or a teacher like Christian Neefe, who was instrumental in achieving the publication of three sonatas by his 13-year-old student Beethoven. No one supervised the studies of the teenager Haydn, who fought homelessness and starvation after he was dismissed (because his voice changed) from the choir of St. Stephen's Cathedral in Vienna. Yet he acquired sufficient technique to accompany singing lessons, teach keyboard instruments, and serve as an organist.

He was an acceptable fiddler and made some money as a street musician and with a dance band. He was proficient enough to play a quartet with Dittersdorf, Mozart and Wanhal. It is true he was not a piano virtuoso, but he acquired a solid enough technique to enable him to accept advanced students. Haydn was, musically speaking, a self-made man. "I had no real teacher," he declared, and he told his biographer Georg Albert Griesinger: "I was no wizard on any instrument, but I knew the potentialities and effects of all. I was not a bad pianist and singer and was also able to play a violin concerto." Even so, he had a keen understanding of keyboard idioms. He adapted his keyboard writing to the layout of the hands much more so than has been generally recognized or acknowledged.

Haydn's life was more humdrum and uneventful than that of his contemporary, Mozart, and there was less to attract the attention of the public. There are qualities in Haydn's music that suggest that his approach to composition also was more introspective and less impulsive. The possibilities of thematic development were of particular interest to Haydn; often a comparatively short sonata movement may have a development section that is not only surprisingly expansive, but proves to be the emotional climax of the movement as well. In many ways Haydn's work is indicative of a genius that matured not with the swiftness and brilliance of, say, Mozart's, but with a more gradual and deliberate increase of strength. Haydn's piano sonatas are the ideal genre through which to view that maturation.

Haydn the Keyboard Composer

Haydn was perhaps the most "modern" composer of all Western musical history—meaning that he was able to feel the pulse of musical taste throughout his long, creative life and enlarge upon it. His activities as a composer of keyboard sonatas covered about half a century, from the 1750s to the 1790s. It was a period of varying musical styles—the twilight of the grand style of the late Baroque meeting its opposite: music for connoisseurs versus music for amateurs; music of an expressive, individual style and its counterpart, music mainly for exercise or unpretentious entertainment. His music emerged in the late Baroque and evolved into the developing Romantic style of the young Beethoven and Schubert.

Haydn's piano sonatas were very popular in his day. The word "favorite" appeared frequently on the covers of the numerous editions of selected sonatas that were published throughout Europe and the United States.

A close acquaintance with these sonatas reveals one of the most outstanding original masters of his art. The qualities of these sonatas are similar to those that distinguish Haydn's string quartets and symphonies; chief among these are a rhythmic freedom and an absence of "squareness" in rhythmic structure, humor, wealth of ideas, and abundance of invention.

Haydn's keyboard works are finally being recognized as a major contribution to the piano repertoire. Indeed, some of these sonatas are masterpieces that display astonishing formal and stylistic diversity and cast their shadows into the 19th century.

The Piano Sonatas

Haydn's piano sonatas were written over a period extending from the years of earliest activity until 1795. They provide a fascinating record of the development of his style and artistic personality. For Haydn, as for Beethoven, the piano sonata was the proving ground throughout his career where he could experiment, then apply what he had learned to the quartet and symphony. It is remarkable how steadfastly and purposefully this modest man, who was at the same time an artist of the highest integrity, developed his talents.

The early sonatas, those written up to around 1766, testify to a heroic effort on Haydn's part to proceed beyond the limitations of the divertimento, which dominated Austrian instrumental music at the time. This largely self-taught young composer wanted discursive musical logic—that is, development—not mere entertainment. Even at this early stage of his creative career, the asymmetrical themes, the irregular sentence structure, the variety of formal designs, and the palpable effort at thematic consistency were beyond the powers of most of his colleagues.

Haydn called his early sonatas (written for his own keyboard students) partitas and divertimentos. (The 19th- and 20th-century editions of partitas and divertimentos dispensed with these terms and applied to these compositions the designation "sonata" instead.) Partita is synonymous with suite, and divertimento is a category of its own. Literally translated, the word means "entertainment," and applied to music, it denotes music of a light character, as opposed to the "learned" style of the Baroque, with its contrapuntal and fugal complexities. The application of these terms to Haydn's first keyboard works in two, three, and four movements indicates the character of the music. Light and entertaining qualities preclude the use of the minor key, and it is highly significant that Haydn composed his first sonata (to be labeled as such) in a minor key (C minor) in 1771. The choice of tonality was, no doubt, a reflection of the "Sturm und Drang" (storm and stress) that was beginning to be felt culturally at the time.

With the works in the 1770s we enter the period of Haydn's wide-ranging experimentation, and the variety, especially in formal design, is considerable, even fantastic. The romantic effusiveness of the sonatas of this period shows the influence of C. P. E. Bach, but the agitated tone and the dark hues of the music are nevertheless disciplined by a compelling logic of thematic development; Beethoven learned much from these works. The desire for variation and the refusal to repeat verbatim are the strongest among Haydn's instincts, and the inventiveness in his period construction is perhaps the most original of the great Viennese Classical trinity of Haydn, Mozart and Beethoven.

The middle-period sonatas of the 1780s display a marked increase in piano virtuosity. Although Haydn was not a keyboard virtuoso, his writing of this period shows the influence of his friends Marianna and Katharina von Auenbrugger, keyboard players whose playing and insight, he said, "equal that of the greatest masters." The "Sturm und Drang" crisis having occurred in symphony, string quartet, and sonata alike, Haydn now settled down to the serene, Classical style that was largely his own creation.

He soon mastered the characteristic forms that make up the Classical sonata—the opening allegro, the minuet, the largo/adagio, and the sonata-rondo finale, which became a primary vehicle of Haydnesque exuberance and wit.

Especially from the Auenbrugger sonatas (Hob. XVI/35–39, composed during the 1770s) onward, Haydn began to develop an expressive, personal tone, more sophisticated harmony, fluid and integrated counterpoint, and original formal designs. In these works we begin to feel the subtle influence of Mozart displacing that of C. P. E. Bach. "Haydn's highly original procedures are not 'justified' by any

of the rules and standards decreed in our theory books, and literal analysts have a difficult time forcing his imaginative 'irregularities' ('loose style,' the north German contemporaries called it) into any set pattern." [1]

The last three sonatas (Hob. XVI/50–52), composed in London during his second visit there in 1794–95, are, like the late quartets and symphonies, the epitome of the Classical style. There is a strong inclination toward monothematic sonata construction; Haydn now uses the entire range of the keyboard, and we observe an absence of the popular, public-pleasing tone of the divertimento—we have entered the early Romantic world of the young Beethoven.

Keyboard Instruments in Haydn's Time

What keyboard instruments did Haydn use when composing these sonatas? He composed during the twilight era of the transition from harpsichord to fortepiano (the early piano). It seems that all of the sonatas up to 1766 were intended for the harpsichord (perhaps even the clavichord), yet the writing is essentially pianistic in conception. It is impossible to determine just when he began to conceive his compositions for the fortepiano *(hammerklavier)* only. It appears, however, that with the Sonata in B-flat, Hob. XVI/18, composed around 1766–67, the writing is more completely of the character one finds in 18th-century compositions that are definitely for the fortepiano. This observation is supported by the fact that in Haydn's own catalog this work is listed as a *Sonata pour la Pianoforte*. The editor agrees with Christa Landon, who said that "the entire question of what instrument to use seems . . . to be primarily

of historical interest and one whose importance is generally exaggerated. The essential musical substance of a masterpiece is quite independent of such considerations, which in themselves will always vary with changing taste and local acoustic conditions." [2] Nevertheless, so firmly was the fortepiano entrenched as the 18th century drew to a close that Haydn, in 1790, said he was no longer in the habit of playing the harpsichord, and he advised a friend to get a fortepiano.

Performing on the fortepiano differs greatly from performing on the modern grand piano. Less arm weight and wrist action are required, but at the same time, finger movement must be more clearly articulated than is customary today; thus passagework is more detached and less legato than is generally regarded as ideal today. These ideas should be kept in mind when performing these sonatas on a modern piano.

1. Paul Henry Lang, "Haydn at the Keyboard," *High Fidelity* (January 1977), p. 108.

2. Preface to Haydn, *The Complete Piano Sonatas*, edited by Christa Landon, Vienna: Universal Edition, 1963, pp. XVII–XVIII.

Ornamentation

Haydn's ornamentation was influenced by two different traditions: the North German, represented by C. P. E. Bach's *Essay on the True Art of Playing Keyboard Instruments* (1753), and the South German and Austrian, as exemplified by Leopold Mozart's *Treatise on the Fundamental Principles of Violin Playing* (1756). The great variety of Haydn's music forces us to conclude that his ornaments are not to be executed with rigid adherence to one set of rules, but can often be performed in different ways. The following are the most frequently used ornaments in the sonatas:

I. Small-note appoggiatura *(Vorschlag):* Generally played on the beat, to be slurred to the main note; can be long or short.

a. Long: usually takes half the value of the main note (one-third or two-thirds the value when the main note is dotted).

b. Short: usually quick and unaccented.

c. In the case of an appoggiatura followed by a rest, the resolving note should be sounded in place of the rest.

Sonata in G, Hob. XVI/6, Minuet, measure 28

d. There are also appoggiaturas that should be played as upbeats and lightly (like grace notes), as in the first movement of the Sonata in D, Hob. XVI/37, measures 1, 5–6, 17–18, etc.

measure 5

measure 17

measure 18

II. Trill: *tr*, *t* ～～～, ～～

Long and short trills begin on the beat and generally start with the upper neighbor. Sometimes they begin on the main note; trills that have appoggiaturas from either above or below begin on the main note.

Sonata in E Minor, Hob. XVI/34, 3rd movement, measures 1–4

In most cases Haydn's trills are to be played with two terminating notes *(Nachschlag)*, whether notated or not, in the same tempo as the trill.

The sign ～～ is usually used for short trills (sometimes called inverted mordents) but not invariably. It consists of three notes and begins on the main note.

Sonata in E-flat, Hob. XVI/38, 1st movement, measure 1

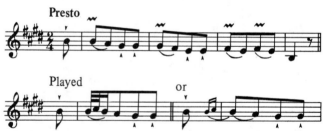

Sonata in E, Hob. XVI/31, Presto, measures 1–4

That this execution was intended by Haydn is clear from many passages in his works where the short trill ～～ is written out in large or small notes, as in the following example:

Sonata in G, Hob. XVI/39, 1st movement, measure 18

III. Mordent:
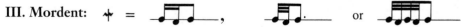

The mordent must always be played on the beat.

IV. Turn:

This has been called "The Haydn Ornament." In a letter to his publisher Artaria, of December 10, 1785, Haydn specifically differentiated between ∞ and ⃰ (= ⃰?), calling the latter a "half mordent." But autograph evidence indicates that Haydn used ⃰ instead of ∞, or vice versa, in parallel passages.

The chart below[3] discusses the turn as it is typically indicated in Haydn's music:

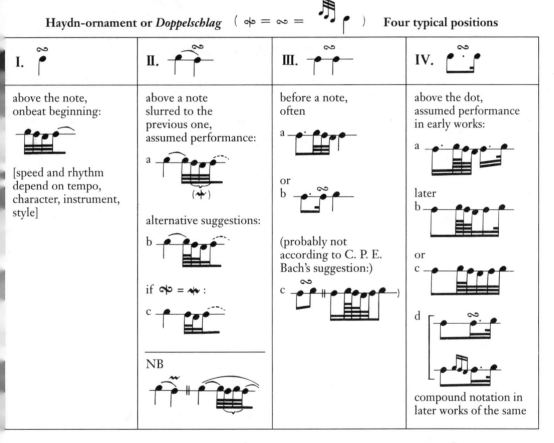

a. The sign ⃰ plus an appoggiatura   probably indicates

b. The two signs ∞ and ⃰ used together indicate a trill with closing notes.

V. Trill with turn: ⃰

(Same realization as in IV above.)

3. László Somfai, "How to Read and Understand Haydn's Notation in Its Chronologically Changing Concepts," *Internationaler Joseph Haydn Kongress, Wien 1982*, p. 30.

VI. Turn and trill: ∿

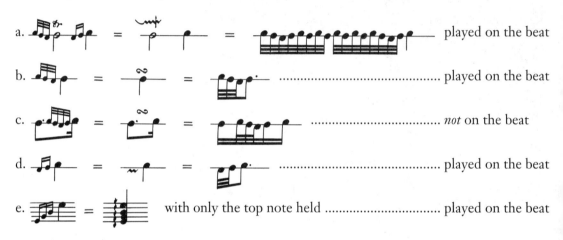

VII. Groups of small notes: These are frequently semi-realizations of ornaments. They, therefore, should be interpreted in the same way as the ornaments. Thus:

a. .... played on the beat

b. .... played on the beat

c. .... *not* on the beat

d. .... played on the beat

e. ... with only the top note held .... played on the beat

VIII. Arpeggio:

This indicates a simple rolling of the chord from bottom to top. More chords are to be arpeggiated than Haydn indicated. Thus, even in many cases where no arpeggiation is indicated, the choice to arpeggiate is available to the performer. Arpeggios for the right hand are almost always to be played on the beat and with accentuation of the top note.

Sonata in E-flat, Hob. XVI/49, 1st movement, measures 106–107

These suggestions show that ornaments can occasionally be substituted for one another in Haydn's keyboard music. Often the choice as to whether to play a turn, a short trill or a regular trill is left to the performer, who should select the ornament best suited to the musical context of the passage; the tempo and character of the movement itself being decisive. The sporadic and inconsistent ornament notation left by Haydn also suggests that the performer should add ornaments, especially in slow cantabile movements. Frequently the ornamentation should be increased or varied when sections of a movement are repeated. However, care must be taken to not obscure the quiet and clear motion of a melodic line with too many ornaments.

Portrait of Haydn
by L. Guttenbrunn

Phrasing and Articulation

The wedge-shaped dash (𝅘𝅥) used by Haydn indicates any type of staccato, or an accent, or combination of both. It does not mean a staccatissimo, as in Beethoven's later usage. Haydn used dots, either slurred (𝅘𝅥 𝅘𝅥 𝅘𝅥)
or
unslurred (𝅘𝅥 𝅘𝅥 𝅘𝅥),
for mezzo staccatos, especially in groups of repeated notes. Unfortunately, it is not always possible to distinguish a dot from a dash in the manuscript; consequently engravers and copyists frequently misread them. In some cases, the performer must decide whether dots or dashes are more appropriate for the musical situation. In this edition, all articulation marks in parentheses are editorial—therefore, the pianist can decide whether to use editorial assistance or not.

A slur can mean either:

           = legato slur

or   = articulation slur

Many passages and movements contain no articulation marks. The pianist must add them. To identify the articulation of a phrase, think of how a string player would bow the passage or how a singer would sing it—then sing, hum or whistle it. This will show the phrase's melodic contour and climax, and the places where natural breaks occur. In general, stepwise movement tends to be legato and disjunct movement nonlegato—though there are many exceptions to this.

Pedaling

Haydn left only two pedal indications in all of his keyboard music; these occur in the first movement of the Sonata in C, Hob. XVI/50, where an exceptionally atmospheric and mysterious effect is required. These indications are identified in footnotes. The pedalings are marked not because these passages are the only places where Haydn desired pedal, but because they create unusual effects. The editor has added pedal indications sparingly, keeping in mind that all fortepianos of the last three decades of the 18th century were equipped with a knee lever to raise and lower the dampers much the same as the modern piano's damper pedal does. In using the damper pedal on today's instruments, the pianist should remember that in Haydn's piano music clarity of articulation, texture and phrasing must never be obscured. The pedal, when used in playing Haydn, must be imperceptible and therefore must be changed very frequently. The una corda (soft) pedal should be used to extend the available range of tone colors, not to disguise the pianist's inability to produce a pianissimo.

Dynamics

Haydn used **pp** and **ff** very rarely, but they are most significant when they do occur. His basic dynamic marks were **p** and **f**, and the contrast between them is of major importance. They represent a greater variety of dynamic levels than they do today, for *mf* (mezzo forte—rather loud) was in his day unusual, **pf** (poco forte—somewhat loud) and mezza voce (inwardly) rarer still, and *mp* (mezzo piano) nonexistent. Thus, there must be dynamic inflections within the basic piano and forte categories. It is sometimes necessary for the performer to add a crescendo or decrescendo between the two levels. Haydn sometimes used **f** to indicate an expressive rather than a true forte. (See Sonata in G, Hob. XVI/40, in Vol. III, first movement, measures 3 and 4: the **f** seems to imply an expressive stress within the prevailing **p** rather than a true forte.)

The sforzato sign (*fz*) was used frequently by Haydn and may be interpreted in a variety of ways: (1) as a sharp rhythmic accent, especially in fast movements; (2) as an expressive, hesitating, or soft key attack; (3) as an indication for the use of rubato in slow and/or fast movements.

Many of these sonatas contain no dynamics, which was not unusual for this period. Performers were expected to add the inflections natural to their instruments—the clavichord, fortepiano and harpsichord providing, as they do, completely different tonal resources. To prove this point, the Minuet and Trio of the Sonata in A, Hob. XVI/26, contains no dynamics in the original edition. Yet this same movement, when it reappears in the Symphony No. 47 in D, is full of dynamics. Why? Multiple players could not perform effectively without them. So Haydn surely expected a soloist to add dynamics to the keyboard version and also to other unmarked movements as well, but he left the details up to the performer according to the resources of his instrument.

Today's performer should use as models the works Haydn did mark with dynamics. Having assimilated these, the performer should be able to arrive at a dynamic plan in the unmarked movements and to flesh out the often sparse and random dynamic indications that appear in others. It is for these reasons that the editor has added numerous dynamic marks in this edition, always enclosed in parentheses within each page. They are only suggestions and the performer should feel no compulsion to use them.

Chronology and Authenticity

"I acknowledge with pleasure the desire of many music lovers to own a complete edition of my piano compositions, which is, I feel, a flattering indication of their approval, and I shall see to it that in this collection no work which wrongly bears my name will be included." So begins the foreword, drafted by Gottfried Christoph Härtel and signed by Haydn on December 20th, 1799, that appeared in Volume I of the so-called Haydn *Oeuvres complettes* (which was neither complete nor chronological) issued by Breitkopf & Härtel between 1800 and 1806.

Chronology and authenticity have been pursued and established to the best of the abilities of a number of outstanding scholars, but unanimity can never be reached on these matters: the ascriptions and dates of many of Haydn's youthful works will always remain conjectural. We probably have not yet seen all of Haydn's early keyboard works, since they were written for his students rather than for the general public. Even as late as 1961 part of one (Hob. XVI/5) appeared at an auction in Marburg, Germany. Hopefully, others of the "lost sonatas" known from Haydn's own catalog will eventually come to light.

Sonata No. 15, Hob. XVI/15, is not included in the present edition since it is a dubious arrangement for piano of the Divertimento in C (Hob. II/11) for flute, oboe and strings that did not originate with Haydn.

Sonata No. 17, Hob. XVI/17, is not included in the present edition as it has definitely been identified as having been composed by the Braunschweig Kapellmeister Johann Schwanenberg (1740–1804).

Sonata in G, Hob. XVI/G1, is included because of its stylistic unity. The first movement of the Sonata in G, Hob. XVI/11, also appears as the last movement of the Sonata in G, Hob. XVI/G1, where it fits more appropriately.

Sonata in D, Hob. XVII/D1, is included because of its three movements, which makes it seem closer to a sonata than a *Klavierstück*.

Sonata in E-flat, Hob. XVI/Es2, which was discovered in 1962, is included. Another sonata discovered at the same time, the Sonata in E-flat, Hob. XVI/Es3, is not included, since an old copy of this work appeared in 1972 with Mariano Romano listed as the composer. This sonata also does not seem to be up to the high level of Haydn's craftsmanship.

Each sonata lists its known or presumed approximate date of composition.

About This Edition

This edition is a practical urtext-pedagogical edition designed with the idea of performing these works on the modern piano. The editor believes that the full color and subtlety of these sonatas can be effectively realized on a modern piano of suitable character. Indeed, this music is beautifully congenial to the modern piano since the sustained quality often demanded is fairly easy to produce on a modern instrument. "Banging" as well as "tinkling" should be avoided, and the power of the concert grand can be scaled down without hurting the quality of the sound.

Most of the sonatas in Volume I are especially appropriate for the progressing intermediate student. Haydn wrote many of these sonatas for his pupils and patrons, and the dedications of the music are one good guide to their intended style. These works can serve as an effective introduction for the intermediate pianist to the great Viennese Classical style, which represents for many people the pinnacle of musical achievement in Western civilization. Indeed, these three volumes of Haydn's piano sonatas contain some of the most precious music we have inherited. While scrupulously respecting the original text, this edition offers many valuable, stylistically faithful suggestions for interpretation.

As previously mentioned, Haydn left pedal indications in only the first movement of the Sonata in C, Hob. XVI/50. Thus all other pedal markings are editorial. Pedaling is sparingly indicated so that no sound sustains when it should not. These pedal indications are only suggestions and must not be adhered to slavishly. There are many instances where touches of pedal can be used, but these vary so much according to the instrument, room acoustics, etc., that only the performer can decide when to use the pedal quickly and imperceptibly. Only careful listening can dictate musical pedaling.

This edition is based on the Karl Päsler edition from *Serie 14: Klavierwerke*, n.d. (actually 1918), of the Breitkopf & Härtel (Leipzig) Haydn complete-works edition inaugurated in 1907 under the general editorship of Eusebius Mandyczewsky. Päsler included 52 sonatas in his edition. He also listed eight sonatas thought to be lost, the themes of which were recorded by Haydn in his catalog, the so-called *Entwurf-Katalog*. Päsler, however, did not include these eight works in his chronological listing of the 52. This chronological arrangement of the Breitkopf & Härtel edition was subsequently taken over by Anthony von Hoboken in his Haydn Catalog,[4] so that the Hoboken numbers are identical with those of Päsler. Also consulted for textual differences were the Vienna Urtext Edition, edited by Christa Landon (1963) and the Henle edition, edited by Georg Feder (1971). The L. (Landon) numbers are listed for each sonata.

All fingerings are by the editor except those italicized in the sonatas Hob. XVI/42, first movement, measure 23, and Hob. XVI/45, third movement, measure 20 (Vol. III), which are Haydn's.

To assist the teacher and performer, four categories of grading (intermediate, late intermediate, early advanced, advanced) are used that generally correspond to the accepted divisions of difficulty. No grading can be absolute, however, and the assignment of a grade category does not mean that all pieces of the same category are equally interchangeable. Choices must be made according to the musical development, technical ability and maturity of the performer.

Editorial additions appear in parentheses. Numerous ornaments are realized either in footnotes or the score. All metronome indications are editorial.

---

4. Joseph Haydn. *Thematisch-bibliographisches Werkverzeichnis zusammen gestellt von Anthony von Hoboken.* B. Schott's Söhne, Mainz, 1957.

The editor wishes to thank the following libraries and institutions for their assistance in the preparation of this edition: the Musiksammlung der Oesterreichischen Nationalbibliothek, Vienna; the Sammlungen der Gesellschaft der Musikfreunde, Vienna; the Department of Music History of the Moravian State Museum, Brno; the Musikbibliothek der Stadt, Leipzig; and the Department of Manuscripts of the British Museum, London.

About the Sonatas

Allegro: Lively and motoric; motivic repetition needs melodic shaping; Alberti bass should be carefully subdued. *Andante:* Elegant melody needs sensitive shaping of phrases. *Minuet* and *Trio:* Light-hearted Minuet, darker Trio. Each movement of this sonata is completely different, but they form a cohesive unit. Late intermediate.

Allegro: Five-finger patterns require careful articulation; keep Alberti bass subdued. *Minuet* and *Trio:* Simple, charming, unpretentious. *Finale:* Contains contrasting styles and figuration; middle section in parallel minor. This piece is also used as the opening movement of the Sonata in G, Hob. XVI/11. Intermediate.

Moderato: Varied textures and two-note groupings; requires special sensitivity to phrasing and voicing. *Largo* (G minor): Complex rhythms require steady pulse; dramatic aria style. *Minuet* and *Trio:* Lively Minuet contrasts with more somber Trio. Early advanced.

Allegretto: Subtle dynamic and articulative nuances are required for successful performance. *Andante* (G major): Stately, complex rhythms; requires melodic shaping and awareness of contrapuntal lines. *Minuet* and *Trio:* Trio undergoes mood changes, beautifully shaped phrases. Late intermediate.

Moderato: Many virtuosic figurations require careful attention to melodies embedded in them; consistent tempo necessary. *Minuet* and *Trio:* Stately Minuet, more subdued Trio; dotted notes and triplets can cause problems. Intermediate.

Allegro: Brilliant and energetic; demands dexterity. *Minuet* and *Trio:* Mood of Trio requires big dynamic change from Minuet. *Presto:* More difficult than it looks; mode changes reflect varied characters. Most authorities question the authenticity of this sonata. If it is authentic, it must be one of Haydn's earliest works. Early advanced.

Allegro: Varied rhythmic diversity including shifted beat division, fast trills and scales; carefully worked-out dynamics and articulation will add much interest. *Minuet* and *Trio:* Dotted rhythms must be precise; Trio alternates duplets and triplets; dynamic echoes and melodic shaping can add much interest. *Adagio* (G minor): Florid melodies full of lyrical beauty; left-hand melody in thirds requires special attention. *Finale:* Fast scales and arpeggios make this a brilliant movement. Early advanced.

Thema (Moderato): The melody is the main subject of variation in this set of three variations, as the bass line and harmonies remain the same throughout; arpeggios and triplet 16ths are the main technical problems. *Minuet:* Graceful and full of melodic charm; clear texture, elegant phrase balance. *Finale* (Allegro): Brilliant, full of mordents, virtuosic with hand crossings, fast scales, octaves, but still accessible. Sounds more difficult than it is. An excellent recital movement. Late intermediate.

Allegro moderato: Weak-finger trills; brisk character requires creative dynamics and articulation. *Minuet* and *Trio:* Tuneful, scalar figuration is not easy; Trio requires careful left-hand melodic voicing. *Finale:* Most difficult movement; lively character requires much attention to detail; two notes against three; numerous broken octaves. Late intermediate.

Allegro: Tricky rhythmic problems such as offbeat patterns and triplets surrounded by duplets. *Minuet:* Complex rhythms, broken triads and ornaments. *Andante:* This well-balanced, melodic movement includes contrapuntal lines, scales and ornaments. *Allegro:* Requires good finger independence and facility. The key of G major is frequently treated by Haydn in a lighthearted, witty manner, sometimes with a "country idyll" character. Intermediate.

Allegro: This lively movement resembles Scarlatti, and contains attractive virtuosic figuration. *Minuet:* Keep light, in spite of the numerous octaves. Each contrapuntal line should be heard independently. *Scherzo:* Very pianistic; subdued left-hand 16ths; interesting broken intervals and scalar passages. Late intermediate.

Moderato: Beethoven-like relationship between first and second subjects; requires varied touches and dynamics; taxing ornaments. Maintain a relaxed tempo. *Minuet* and *Trio:* Colorful Minuet contrasted with a darkly expressive Trio. *Finale:* Spirited, fast figuration requires close attention to fingering; stress the numerous countermelodies. Late intermediate.

Presto: This movement is exactly the same as the last movement of the Sonata in G, Hob. XVI/G1. Requires light octaves, good finger facility, and sensitive dynamic changes, especially in the second half. *Andante:* In sonata-allegro form; graceful phrase structure requires expressive nuance. *Minuet:* Rustic character; feel pulse in one beat. Stop the trills in measures 4, 12, and 20 after about one quarter note. Late intermediate.

Andante: Reminiscent of early Mozart; long trills and other ornaments should be graceful and elegant; dynamic shape of melodic lines requires utmost sensitivity. *Minuet* and *Trio:* Cheerful and innocent, while the Trio is dramatic and polyphonic in texture. *Finale:* Motivic, Alberti bass, clever figuration, delightful throughout. Late intermediate.

Moderato: Taut and angular; requires creative articulation as well as rhythmic precision; numerous ornaments. *Minuet* and *Trio:* Change fingers on the repeated notes; the Trio is especially delightful. *Finale:* Brilliant and jovial; varied figurations are not difficult; parallel thirds; requires evenness and finger independence. Late intermediate.

Haydn's fortepiano, in the room in which he died

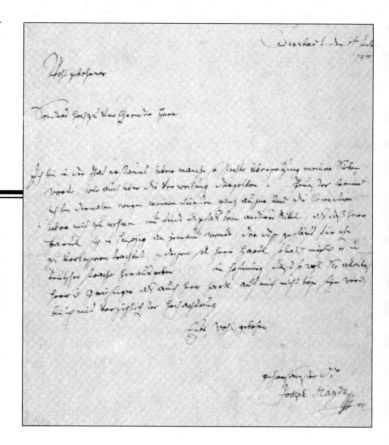

Sonata in D, Hob. XVI/14; L. 16
(before 1766) ....Page 104

Allegro moderato: Fluent passagework in shifting rhythms; winsome and expansive; fuller treatment of development section than in earlier sonatas. The frequent rubato (see measures 10, 12, 65 to 73, etc.), expressive character and delicate figurations demand a moderate tempo. *Minuet:* Lighthearted; more serious *Trio;* unusual harmonies. *Finale:* Many opportunities for contrast; pianistic; varied figurations. Haydn experiments with unusual phrase lengths: five instead of the usual four. Early advanced.

Sonata in E-flat, Hob. XVI/16
(before 1766) ....Page 112

The authenticity of this sonata is doubtful because of its stylistic inconsistency. The opening *Andante* movement is constructed in binary form with two parallel sections in each part: an opening *Andante* connected by a cadenza to a fast section. The musical material is not as polished as one usually finds in Haydn. *Minuet:* Varied rhythms. *Trio:* In relative minor, exploits crossing hands. *Presto:* Lively, attractive scale and broken-chord figuration. Intermediate.

Sonata in B-flat, Hob. XVI/18; L. 20
(around 1766–67) ....Page 117

Allegro moderato: Unusual harmony; numerous ornaments must be performed within a small area of the beat; constantly shifting rhythm between 16th and 32nd notes. Must have steady tempo and effective dynamics. *Moderato:* Introspective, minuet influence, contrapuntal textures. Advanced.

Sonata in D, Hob. XVI/19; L. 30
(1767) ....Page 126

Moderato: Bold and dramatic; several themes developed and unified; contains rhythmic vitality and concertante elements. *Andante:* Lyrical; the juxtaposition of high and low registers should be emphasized by careful contrast of different tone colors and dynamics. Requires imaginative articulation. A cadenza could be added at measure 112. *Finale:* Combines qualities of a lighthearted scherzo with variation form, and a brilliant ending. An outstanding sonata, with each movement of equal strength. Early advanced.

Sonata in C Minor, Hob. XVI/20; L. 33
(1771) ....Page 140

This is the first work to use the term "sonata." Earlier ones were originally called partitas or divertimentos. This sonata exhibits a major transition from clavichord to authentic piano style. *Moderato:* Has a powerful intensity, changing textures, uneven groupings, long development, many dynamic marks from Haydn; requires creative articulation. *Andante con moto:* Exploits extreme registers between the hands; written-out rubato (measures 14–20, 31–37, etc.); the high F at measure 53 was the highest key on Haydn's keyboard at the time. In playing syncopated lines at measures 14–19 and 31–35, try to avoid a constant cross-reference of "note against note" between the main lines. Rather, the pianist should try to perform quasi-independent lines, as if two musicians were performing their parts without coordination. As an exercise, play both lines simultaneously, or even play the melody one eighth note earlier than written. *Finale:* Solemn tonality of C minor pervades this movement as well as the first; first subject recaptures the powerful intensity of the first movement. The exposition presents a sequence of motivic periods, well combined, but only in the middle part of the movement are their hidden forces revealed in a fascinating, almost fantasylike development and recapitulation. This is one of the three or four greatest sonatas Haydn ever composed. Advanced.

Sonata in E-flat, Hob. XVI/Es2; L. 17
(before 1766)...Page 152

This work was discovered in 1962 by Georg Feder in the collection of the Benedictine Abbey at Rajhrad (now in the Moravske Muzeum in Brno, Moravia, Czechoslovakia). Feder labeled it Es2. This sonata and its companion piece (discussed on page 13) are referred to fictitiously as Hob. XVI/Es2 and Es3 (Es means E-flat in German). They are not cited in Hoboken because his first volume (1957) had already appeared before their discovery. *Moderato:* Alternates dramatic characters; playful, pompous; complex rhythms and ornaments. *Andante* (C minor): Melodic; numerous broken triplet chords; parallel thirds; ornaments must be graceful. *Minuet* and *Trio:* Rhythmic, punctuated by dramatic rests. Trio is contrapuntal and harmonically innovative. Late intermediate.

Sonata in E Minor, Hob. XVI/47; L. 19
(around 1765)...Page 160

Adagio: Poignant, wistful, siciliano that directly links with a driving major tonality in the following movement. *Allegro:* Contrapuntal; opening motive is used as the basis for the most intensive development of a single idea in all of Haydn's keyboard music. *Finale* (Tempo di Minuet): Tightly organized around opening motive. All three movements are unified by their opening motives. Light, elegant dance requires refined style and grace. Early advanced.

For Further Reading

Paul Badura-Skoda. "On Ornamentation in Haydn." *The Piano Quarterly* 135 (Fall 1986) 38–48.

A. Peter Brown. *Joseph Haydn's Keyboard Music.* Bloomington: Indiana University Press, 1986.

Howard Ferguson. *Keyboard Interpretation.* New York & London: Oxford University Press, 1975.

H.C.R. Landon. *Haydn: Chronicle and Works.* 5 vols. Bloomington: Indiana University Press, 1976–80.

Carolyn Maxwell, ed. *Haydn—Solo Piano Literature.* Boulder, CO: Maxwell Music Evaluation, 1983.

Carl Parrish. "Haydn and the Piano." *Journal of the American Musicological Society* I (1948) 27–44.

Charles Rosen. *The Classical Style.* New York: Viking Press, 1971.

Sonata in C

(before 1766)

Hob. XVI/1; L.10

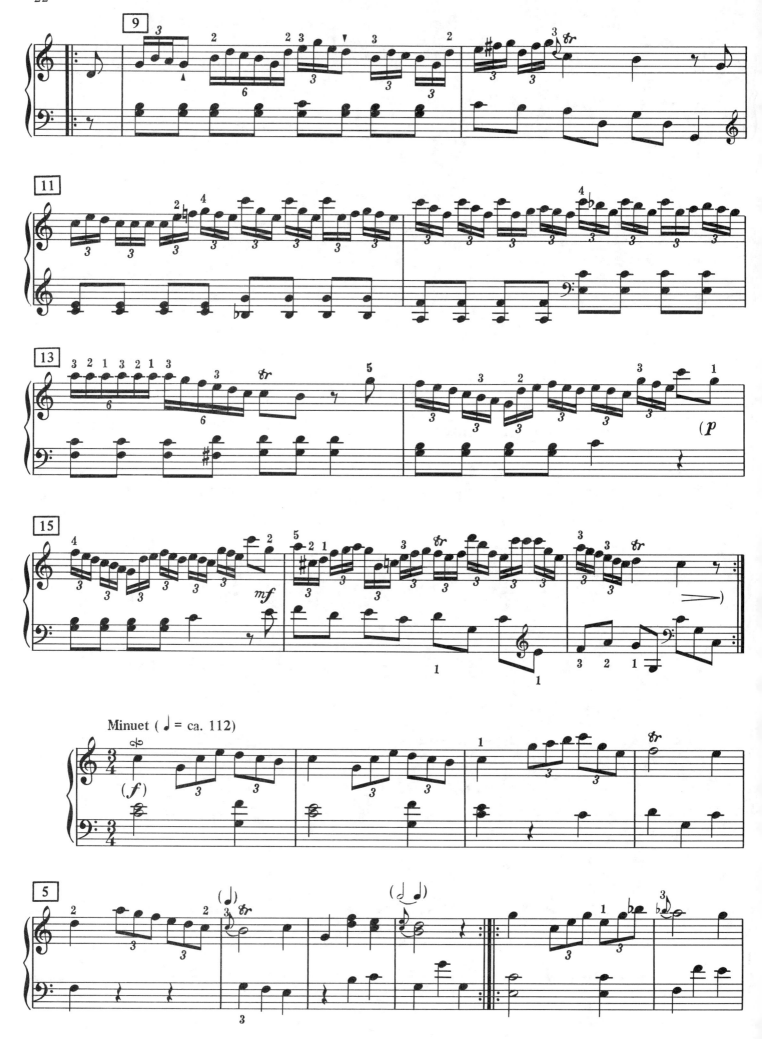

23

Minuet da Capo

Sonata in G

(before 1766)

Hob. XVI/G1; L.4

Allegro (♩ = ca. 108)

26

Minuet da Capo

Sonata in B–flat

(before 1766)

Moderato (♩ = ca. 104)

Hob. XVI/2; L.11

(a) ♫♩. ♩   (b) The editor suggests E♭, but compare measure 112.

© Shorter than

34

Minuet da Capo

Sonata in C
(before 1766)

Hob. XVI/3; L.14

38

42

Minuet (♩ = ca. 144)

ⓔ Stop the trill after about one quarter note. ⓕ

Minuet da Capo

Sonata in D

(around 1765)

Moderato (♩ = ca. 116)

Hob. XVI/4; L.9

ⓐ as at measure 51

46

Minuet da Capo

Sonata in A
(before 1763)

Hob. XVI/5; L.8

52

Minuet (♩ = ca. 126)

Minuet da Capo

53

55

Sonata in G

(before 1766)

Hob. XVI/6; L.13

(a) Other sources show this passage one octave lower.

(b) G# would correspond to C# in measure 45.

58

ⓒ This means to continue the preceding trill.

60

Minuet da Capo

g) A short cadenza is appropriate here.

Finale (♩.= ca. 72)
Allegro molto

Sonata in D
(before 1766)

Hob. XVII/D1; L.7

68

Finale (Allegro) (♩ = ca. 126)

Sonata in C

(before 1766)

Hob. XVI/7; L. 2

71

Minuet da Capo

Finale (♩.= ca. 76)
Allegro

Sonata in G

(before 1766)

Hob. XVI/8; L. 1

Sonata in F

(before 1766)

Hob. XVI/9; L. 3

ⓐ The trills in measures 12, 13, 14, 39, 40, and 41 are better executed as short appoggiaturas.

Minuet (♩ = ca. 120)

Minuet da Capo

Scherzo (♩ = ca. 126)
(Allegro non troppo)

Sonata in C

(before 1766)

Hob. XVI/10; L.6

Minuet (♩ = ca. 120)

Minuet da Capo

83

Sonata in G
(before 1766)

Hob. XVI/11; L.5

Da Capo al Fine

Andante (♩ = ca. 60)

(d) The trill should be stopped after about one quarter note. The turn in measure 12 may be played like a trill.

Minuet da Capo

Sonata in A

(before 1766)

Andante (♪ = ca. 108)

Hob. XVI/12; L.12

Minuet da Capo

Finale (♩. = ca. 80)
(Allegro)

Sonata in E
(before 1766)

Hob. XVI/13; L.15

Minuet da Capo

Finale (♩ = ca. 144)
Presto

103

Sonata in D

(before 1766)

Hob. XVI/14; L.16

Allegro moderato (♩ = ca. 72)

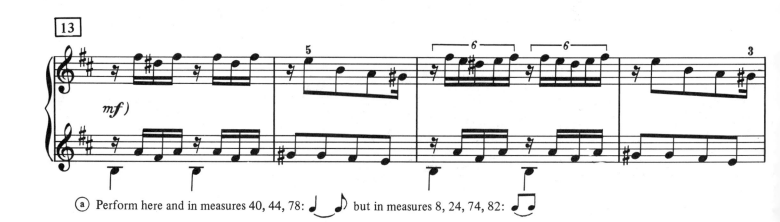

ⓐ Perform here and in measures 40, 44, 78: ♩ ♪ but in measures 8, 24, 74, 82: ♪♪

108

Minuet da Capo

Sonata in E–flat

(before 1766)

Hob. XVI/16

Minuet da Capo

Sonata in B–flat

(around 1766 - 67)

Allegro moderato (♩ = ca. 60)

Hob. XVI/18; L.20

118

120

(d) The trill should be stopped after about an eighth note duration.

Sonata in D
(1767)

Moderato (♩ = ca. 88)

Hob. XVI/19; L.30

130

ⓑ A short cadenza could be added here.

Finale (♩ = ca. 144)
Allegro assai

138

© The repeat sign is contained in the autograph despite the written-out repeat.

Sonata in C Minor
(1771)

Allegro moderato∗
Moderato (♩ = ca. 84)

Hob. XVI/20; L.33

∗First edition

Finale (♩ = ca. 132)
Allegro

150

(h) Perform according to slurs in measures 41-43.

Sonata in E-flat

(before 1766)

Hob. XVI/Es2; L.17

Moderato (♩ = ca. 76)

154

Minuet da Capo

Sonata in E Minor

(around 1765)

Adagio (♩. = ca. 44)

Hob. XVI/47; L.19

Allegro (♩ = ca. 112)

Finale
Tempo di Minuet (♩ = ca. 120)

This page has been purposely left blank.